Trace & Write

Apple

Ant

Axe

apple	ant	axe
apple	ant	axe
apple	ant	axe
apple	ant	axe

Date: ....   Teacher's Signature: ....

B

Trace & Write

| Ball | Banana | Bat |

ball   *banana*   *bat*

ball   *banana*   *bat*

ball   *banana*   *bat*

ball   *banana*   *bat*

Date: ....   Teacher's Signature: ....

C

Trace & Write

| Cat | Cap | Cake |

```
cat        cap        cake

cat        cap        cake

cat        cap        cake

cat        cap        cake
```

Date: .... Teacher's Signature: ....

D

Trace & Write

Dog	Desk	Duck

dog · desk · duck

dog · desk · duck

dog · desk · duck

dog · desk · duck

Date: ....   Teacher's Signature: ....

E

Trace & Write

Elephant **Eraser** **Egg**

elephant   eraser   egg
elephant   eraser   egg
elephant   eraser   egg
elephant   eraser   egg

Date: ....   Teacher's Signature: ....

F

Trace & Write

Fish	Frog	Flower
fish	frog	flower
fish	frog	flower
fish	frog	flower
fish	frog	flower

Date: ....   Teacher's Signature: ....

G

Trace & Write

Goat	Glass	Giraffe

goat   *glass*   *giraffe*

goat   *glass*   *giraffe*

goat   *glass*   *giraffe*

goat   *glass*   *giraffe*

Date: ....   Teacher's Signature: ....

Trace & Write

 Horse	Hen	Helicopter 
horse	hen	helicopter
horse	hen	helicopter
horse	hen	helicopter
horse	hen	helicopter

Date: .... Teacher's Signature: ....

I

Trace & Write

| Igloo | Infant | Ice-cream |

igloo   *infant*   *ice-cream*

igloo   *infant*   *ice-cream*

igloo   *infant*   *ice-cream*

igloo   *infant*   *ice-cream*

Date: ....   Teacher's Signature: ....

J

Trace & Write

Jug	Jelly	Joker

jug   *jelly*   *joker*

jug   *jelly*   *joker*

jug   *jelly*   *joker*

jug   *jelly*   *joker*

Date: .... Teacher's Signature: ....

K

Trace & Write

Kite	Kangaroo	Kingfisher
kite	kangaroo	kingfisher
kite	kangaroo	kingfisher
kite	kangaroo	kingfisher
kite	kangaroo	kingfisher

Date: ....

Teacher's Signature: ....

L

Trace & Write

| Lion | Lamp | Leaf |

lion	lamp	leaf
lion	lamp	leaf
lion	lamp	leaf
lion	lamp	leaf

Date: ....   Teacher's Signature: ....

Trace & Write

| Mango | Mask | Monkey |

mango   mask   monkey

mango   mask   monkey

mango   mask   monkey

mango   mask   monkey

Date: ....   Teacher's Signature: ....

N

Trace & Write

 Nest

 Notebook

 Nuts

nest	notebook	nuts
nest	notebook	nuts
nest	notebook	nuts
nest	notebook	nuts

Date: ....   Teacher's Signature: ....

O

Trace & Write

Owl	Orange	Onion

owl — orange — onion

owl — orange — onion

owl — orange — onion

owl — orange — onion

Date: ....   Teacher's Signature: ....

P

Trace & Write

| Parrot | Pineapple | Pencil |

parrot   *pineapple*   *pencil*

parrot   *pineapple*   *pencil*

parrot   *pineapple*   *pencil*

parrot   *pineapple*   *pencil*

Date: ....   Teacher's Signature: ....

Q

Trace & Write

Quilt   Quill   Queen

quilt   quill   queen

quilt   quill   queen

quilt   quill   queen

quilt   quill   queen

Date: ....   Teacher's Signature: ....

R

Trace & Write

| Rose | Ring | Radish |

rose *ring* *radish*

rose *ring* *radish*

rose *ring* *radish*

rose *ring* *radish*

Date: ....   Teacher's Signature: ....

S

Trace & Write

| Swan | Sandwich | Snake |

swan   sandwich   snake

swan   sandwich   snake

swan   sandwich   snake

swan   sandwich   snake

Date: ....   Teacher's Signature: ....

T

Trace & Write

Tiger

Tomato

Tortoise

tiger	tomato	tortoise
tiger	tomato	tortoise
tiger	tomato	tortoise
tiger	tomato	tortoise

Date: ....   Teacher's Signature: ....

U

Trace & Write

Umbrella

Utensil

Urn

umbrella   utensil   urn

umbrella   utensil   urn

umbrella   utensil   urn

umbrella   utensil   urn

Date: ....   Teacher's Signature: ....

Trace & Write

Van

Violin

Vulture

van   violin   vulture

van   violin   vulture

van   violin   vulture

van   violin   vulture

Date: ....   Teacher's Signature: ....

Trace & Write

| Watch | Wool | Wolf |

watch　　wool　　wolf

watch　　wool　　wolf

watch　　wool　　wolf

watch　　wool　　wolf

Date: .... 　　Teacher's Signature: ....

X

Trace & Write

X-mas tree

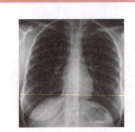
X-ray

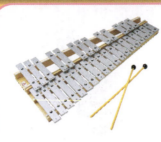
Xylophone

x-mas tree   *x-ray*   *xylophone*

x-mas tree   *x-ray*   *xylophone*

x-mas tree   *x-ray*   *xylophone*

x-mas tree   *x-ray*   *xylophone*

Date: ....   Teacher's Signature: ....

Trace & Write

Yacht

Yo-yo

Yak

yacht   yo-yo   yak

yacht   yo-yo   yak

yacht   yo-yo   yak

yacht   yo-yo   yak

Date: ....   Teacher's Signature: ....

Z

Trace & Write

| Zebra | Zero | Zip |

Zebra — Zebra — Zebra — Zebra

Zero — Zero — Zero — Zero

Zip — Zip — Zip — Zip

Date: .... Teacher's Signature: ....